C000038152

Text: Dennis Kelsall
Series editor: Tony Bowerman
Photographs: Dennis Kelsall, Chatsworth
Estate, Tony Bowerman, James Grant/ www.
jamesgphotography.co.uk, Steve Fedun,
Shutterstock, Dreamstime, Bigstock, iStock

Design: Carl Rogers

© Northern Eye Books Limited 2017

This book contains mapping data licensed from
the Ordnance Survey with the permission of the
Controller of Her Majesty's Stationery Office.
© Crown copyright 2017. All rights reserved.
Licence number 100047867.

| Ordnance Survey Licensed Mapping | Partner |

Northern Eye Books

ISBN 978-1-908632-08-1
A CIP catalogue record for this book is available
from the British Library.

www.northerneyebooks.co.uk

Cover: Chatsworth (Walk 6)
Photograph: © Chatsworth Estate

Important Advice: The routes described in
this book are undertaken at the reader's own
risk. Walkers should take into account their
level of fitness, wear suitable footwear and
clothing, and carry food and water. It is also
advisable to take the relevant OS map with
you in case you get lost and leave the area
covered by our maps.

Whilst every care has been taken to ensure the
accuracy of the route directions, the publish-
ers cannot accept responsibility for errors or
omissions, or for changes in the details given.
Nor can the publisher and copyright owners
accept responsibility for any consequences
arising from the use of this book.

If you find any inaccuracies in either the text or
maps, please write or email us at the address
below. Thank you.

First published in 2014 by
Northern Eye Books Limited
Castle View, High Street, Tattenhall,
Cheshire CH3 9PX

Email: tony@northerneyebooks.com

For sales enquiries, please call 01928 723 744

Twitter: @Northerneyeboo
@Top10walks

Printed & bound in the UK by: Ashford Colour Press

Contents

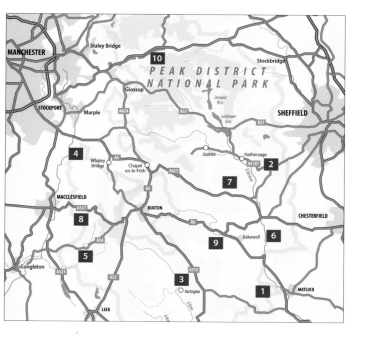

Britain's first National Park

CREATED IN 1951, THE PEAK DISTRICT NATIONAL PARK extends over six counties and is the second most visited of Britain's National Parks. Its highest point lies upon the seemingly remote Kinder plateau, where a mass trespass in 1932 marked the turning point in a long and sometimes bitter campaign that led to the creation of Britain's National Parks and the open access we enjoy today.

The high, peaty moorlands of the northern Dark Peak are founded on gritstone, their stark grandeur accentuated by impressive weatherworn tors and edges. The moors extend out of the Pennines in two horns that enclose the limestone plateau of the White Peak, an upland pasture deeply cleft by narrow gorges and dales. The transition between the two is startlingly abrupt and each has a distinctive character and beauty all its own; the wild openness of the north contrasting with a more intimate landscape dotted with small villages and criss-crossed by old lanes.

Lyme Hall: the grand front

Walking with history

Stone tools from Thor's Cave indicate that man arrived in the Peak as the glaciers receded. More obvious are Bronze and Iron Age circles, burials and earthworks, as well as the scars of mineral extraction — begun by the Romans and continuing today. Some Peakland churches claim Saxon foundation, and by the Middle Ages there was an extensive network of tracks and settlements. Water powered the first industrial revolution, bringing roads, canals and railways, and in the fine country mansions, farmsteads, cottages and town houses there is a rich variety of vernacular and classic architecture.

"Chatsworth! thy stately mansion,

and the pride of thy domain."

William Wordsworth, 1830

TOP 10 **Walks:** Walks with history

TODAY'S PASTORAL SETTING often belies the activity of the past. Yet almost everywhere you go there are traces of man's earlier endeavours that have now become an integral part of the landscape. This collection of walks invites you to step back in time with your imagination to explore some of the historic spots that have helped make the Peak District countryside the rich tapestry that it is today.

BRONZE AGE

Nine Ladies Stone Circle

page 8

IRON AGE

Carl Wark & Higger Tor

page 14

NORMAN

Pilsbury Castle

page 18

MEDIEVAL

Lyme Park

page 24

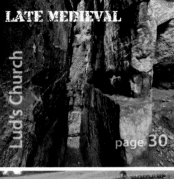

LATE MEDIEVAL

Lud's Church

page 30

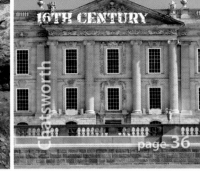

16TH CENTURY

Chatsworth

page 36

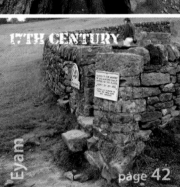

17TH CENTURY

Eyam

page 42

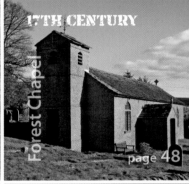

17TH CENTURY

Forest Chapel

page 48

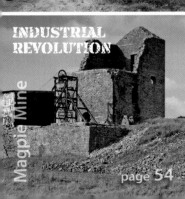

INDUSTRIAL REVOLUTION

Magpie Mine

page 54

VICTORIAN

Longdendale

page 60

Steps up to Rowtor Rocks

Nine Ladies Stone Circle

A prehistoric stone circle and curious cave-like summer-house on Stanton Moor

What to expect:
Field, moor and woodland paths

Distance/time: 7km/ 4½ miles. Allow 2½-3 hours

Start: Beside Druid Inn, Birchover; roadside parking around village

Grid ref: SK 236 621

Ordnance Survey Map: Explorer OL24 *Peak District: White Peak area: Buxton, Bakewell, Matlock & Dove Dale*

After the walk: Druid Inn and Red Lion in Birchover

Walk outline

After exploring Rowtor Rocks behind the Druid Inn, a roundabout route across hillside fields skirts the scattered village. Climbing onto the edge of Stanton Moor, from which there are extensive views, intriguing rock formations and a folly tower line the path to a glade where the Nine Ladies Stone Circle is located. The walk continues through woodland past the site of several abandoned quarries to return to the village.

Nine Ladies Stone Circle

There are a number of prehistoric burial mounds, standing stones and stone circles dotting the area around Stanton Moor, but the Nine Ladies circle is the most impressive. Erected some 3,000 to 4,000 years ago, it dates from the Bronze Age, and although other relics of the period suggest a settled farming community in the area, the meaning and purpose of the circle will perhaps never be known. There are, in fact, ten stones completing the ring, a fallen one was discovered buried in the ground, while another stone, the King Stone, lies a short distance to the south west.

The Cork Stone

Redstart with caterpillar

The Walk

1. Leave the village along a narrow track beside the **Druid Inn**. Just beyond the pub, watch for a path leaving on the right. It climbs behind the pub to the **Rowtor Rocks**, a gritstone outcrop fractured into huge boulders, piled up like some giant's play bricks.

Rooms, passages and chairs sculpted from the rock were conceived by the village's 18th-century vicar Thomas Eyre, who lived at Rowtor Hall and built the village church. Although undoubtedly an ancient site — prehistoric carvings have been discovered on some of the rocks — the connection with Druids is a Victorian fantasy to encourage visitors to the village. Be careful when exploring the site for there are hidden holes and sheer drops.

Return to the track and continue past **St Michael's Church**. Keep ahead by the old vicarage and again where the main track then bends sharply left.

2. Follow an old track that curves round through a gate and stile and past a ruined barn. Reaching a pair of gates and adjacent stile, go through the left gate and, where the path then forks, take the left branch. Climb around the flank of a wooded hill to a gate at the top. The continuing path soon levels, passing a derelict barn that took advantage of an upstanding rock slab for one of its walls. Coming to a junction of paths, keep

Prehistoric meeting place?: *The Nine Ladies stone circle was built in the Bronze Age, around 4,000 years ago*

ahead along the top of a steep bank, shortly passing above **Birchover Wood** and finally joining the end of a track that leads to a narrow lane.

3. Go left, but then turn right in front of **Uppertown Farm**. The track winds around another couple of farms. After 500 metres, look for a stile next to a gate on the left. Walk away beside the left boundary. Eventually arriving at a crossing of paths, keep ahead through

another stile beside a gate and walk on to **Hill Carr Barn**. Swing left around the building into a yard and then branch right along the edge of a camping field. Continuing beyond the corner, the path emerges onto a lane.

4. Turn right, soon heading downhill. After 300 metres, beside a small lay-by, a path leaves onto the National Trust's **Stanton Moor Edge**. The path rises alongside a fence onto the heath, shortly reaching a stile, where to the right, a path leads to a striking rock and commanding viewpoint over the

Under a rock: *The curious rock shelter beneath Rowtor Rocks*

Derwent Valley. Return to the main path and continue beside the fence. At the eventual corner, a path off right leads to the **Cat Stone**. Resuming with the main path it then takes you past a **tower**, *built by the lord of the manor, William Pole Thornhill to celebrate the passing of the Reform Act in 1832.*

Carry on a little farther, shortly coming to a stile. Climb over and head through the trees to intersect a crossing trail opposite the **Nine Ladies Stone Circle**.

5. After exploring the circle, return to the track and follow it left (northeast), soon reaching a gate. Turn back sharp left on a path beside the fence. At its corner, keep with the path ahead for another 300 metres into birch wood grazing. Reaching a faint fork (*SK 246 633*), bear left. The way soon becomes more distinct and rises onto the open heather moor. After passing above a succession of abandoned **quarry pits**, the trail crests the gentle rise of the hill, where the 'trig' column can be seen over to the left. Carry on to a junction of paths by the **Cork Stone**.

6. Turn right, the path dropping to a kissing-gate off the moor and leading

out to a lane. Go left past a working quarry. Just beyond the entrance, turn at a footpath sign into a car park. Cross to a path opposite, which descends the long, wooded snout of **Barton Hill**, where more disused quarries are concealed within the trees. The path ultimately emerges at the bottom onto the lane opposite the **Druid Inn**, completing the walk. ♦

Druids and witchcraft

Although once known across Celtic Europe, the cult of the Druids disappeared under the Romans and little is known of their practices. A Romantic revival during the 18th and 19th centuries erroneously linked the Druids to prehistoric sites such as the Nine Ladies Stone Circle and, of course, Stonehenge. According to local legend, the Nine Ladies were turned to stone for dancing on the sabbath, a fate shared by their fiddler, the King Stone.

Higger Tor sunrise

Carl Wark & Higger Tor

An enigmatic settlement site and stunning edge walk overlooking the wild beauty of the Burbage valley

What to expect:
Moorland paths, moderate climbs

Distance/time: 7km/ 4½ miles. Allow 2 hours

Start: Upper Burbage Bridge car parks, beside A625

Grid ref: SK 259 829

Ordnance Survey Map: Explorer OL1 *The Peak District: Dark Peak area: Kinder Scout, Bleaklow, Black Hill & Ladybower Reservoir*

After the walk: The Norfolk Arms, Ringinglow

Walk outline

A path along the western flank of the Upper Burbage valley takes the walk first onto Higger Tor and then descends to the lower neighbouring outcrop of Carl Wark. Dropping to the base of the valley, it then follows Burbage Brook to the main road near Burbage Bridge. The return climbs onto the edge of Burbage Moor above old quarries to end with a magnificent view across the valley from Burbage Rocks.

Carl Wark

Despite its prominent position and impressive defences, little is actually known about Carl Wark. Although once considered to be an Iron Age fortification, evidence is inconclusive and suggested dates now range from the Bronze Age, contemporary with nearby field systems and burial mounds, to the Saxon period, when the local *Pecsaete* tribes were brought within the kingdom of Mercia. The site occupies a promontory overlooking the valley, naturally defended on three sides by rocky cliffs. The western flank is protected by a massive, 10 metre-high drystone and turf rampart. The place may never have been permanently occupied, but simply a defensible retreat for people and livestock in times of trouble.

Heading for Higger Tor

Bee on heather

The Walk

1. Leave the western **Upper Burbage Bridge car park** through a kissing-gate, taking the rightmost of the two diverging signed paths. **Higger Tor** soon comes into view, the path dropping before a final pull onto the rocky plateau. Although the route follows the top of the cliffs defining the eastern edge,

the summit rocks invite exploration to discover the best views.

2. Drop from the plateau at its south eastern corner, carefully clambering between the boulders to pick up a clear path that heads across the moor to **Carl Wark**. Even from afar, the enormous stone wall guarding its western flank is readily visible. After a short, steep climb onto the top, the rocky platform is worthy of investigation.

3. Head back down the path by which you climbed up to Carl Wark, turning right at the bottom to follow a clear descending path beneath the north eastern face. It runs away across the sloping moor into the valley to meet **Burbage Brook** at an 18th-century **packhorse bridge** by the edge of the forest. Cross the bridge and then a second stream before turning right on a path above the brook. Eventually, the way curves from the stream to intersect a broad sandy path, which you should follow to the right. The path finishes through a couple of gates in a small parking area beside the main road.

4. Take a path on the left out of the car park, which winds through a clump of birch to a gate onto the moor. As you climb away across the bouldery moor, a view opens across the valley to Carl Wark and Higger

Moor and moor: *A clear storm light illuminates Higger Tor*

Tor. Keep ahead at a crossing path, the way rising to gain the edge. Continue above the cliffs of old **quarry workings**.

5. After some 800 metres/½ mile, at the end of the first run of cliffs, bear left at a fork, descending to a cross-path beside a couple of cairns. Carry on ahead, shortly crossing a stream at the base of a gentle fold that drains the moor above. The path then gradually gains height to run along the rim of **Burbage Rocks**. The cliffs ultimately run out as the path approaches the road at **Upper Burbage Bridge**. Turn left back to the car park to complete the walk. ♦

Upper Burbage valley

Once owned by the Duke of Rutland, the valley formed part of a shooting estate centred on nearby Longshaw Lodge. Sheffield Corporation bought the land in the 1920s, intending to build a reservoir. Today, the larch and lodgepole pine forming the plantation above the packhorse bridge attract jays, rooks and chaffinches, while meadow pipits, skylarks and red grouse prefer the open moorland.

A low sun emphasises the mounds and ditches of Pilsbury Castle

Pilsbury Castle

A wander through the higher reaches of the Dove valley to one of the Peak's most evocative castles

What to expect:

Field paths and a couple of lengthy climbs; grille-floored footbridge may be unsuitable for dogs

Distance: 9.5km/ 6 miles. Allow 3 hours

Start: Hartington village pay and display car park

Grid ref: SK 127 602

Ordnance Survey Map: Explorer OL24 *Peak District: White Peak area: Buxton, Bakewell, Matlock & Dove Dale*

After the walk: Pubs, tea rooms and café bar in Hartington, while the Village Store sells tasty pastries and sandwiches

Walk outline

Leaving Hartington, the route climbs an old lane onto the hillside above the River Dove. After easy walking across a succession of grazing pastures flanking Carder Low, the way falls past the farming settlement of Pilsbury to the site of the castle. Descending to cross the river, the return then contours the other side of the valley below Sheen Hill, finally dropping back across the Dove to return to the village.

Pilsbury Castle

Occupying a remote site in the upper reaches of Dove Dale, Pilsbury Castle was built under Henry de Ferrers, one of William of Normandy's followers during the Conquest. It served to control the upper valley of the River Dove, consolidating the Conqueror's ruthless subjugation of this corner of England during which much of what had previously been a relatively prosperous manor was laid waste. Although never rebuilt in stone, the complex earthworks reveal a sizeable fortification that made use of the natural contours and a prominent outcrop of limestone reef within its defences. The castle seems to have been abandoned by the mid-12th century.

Hartington village pond

Early purple orchid

The Walk

1. Leaving the car park, walk into **Hartington**. In the village square, bear

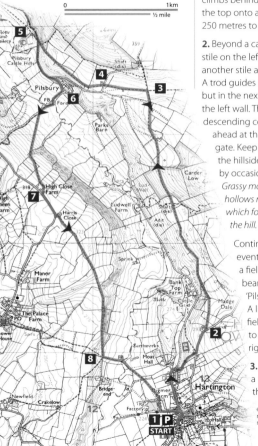

left past the **duck pond** along the lane to 'Pilsbury'. After bending in front of **Moat Hall**, take a track off right. It climbs behind a cottage to emerge at the top onto another lane. Go left for 250 metres to a farm.

2. Beyond a cattle shed, look for a stile on the left. Head past the barn to another stile and keep going to a third. A trod guides you across a pasture, but in the next field turn down beside the left wall. Through a gate, join a descending concrete track, leaving ahead at the bend through another gate. Keep going forwards across the hillside, the way confirmed by occasional blue-topped posts. *Grassy mounds of spoil and irregular hollows reveal an old lead rake, which followed an ore seam across the hill.*

Continue from field to field, eventually passing through a field gate. Ignoring a track, bear right to follow a sign to 'Pilsbury' and 'Crowdecote'. A little farther on, cross a field track and keep ahead to a stile. Drop beside the righthand wall into a dip.

3. Now turn left, joining a path along the base of the valley and ultimately

Limestone country: *Looking across the valley towards Chrome Hill*

leaving over a stile onto a lane near a barn.

4. A sign beside a stile opposite points the ongoing way towards 'Crowdecote'. The path is well marked, shortly reaching a stile beside a gate. Beyond, the ground falls to reveal a lovely view into the upper valley. Walking forward, the castle comes into view, its impressive earthworks laid out below. The path descends to meet a track where a gate opens into **Pilsbury Castle**.

5. Having explored, return to the gate. Turn right beside the wall along the track, which leads out to the sharp bend of a lane. Follow it downhill past **Pilsbury Grange**.

6. Just after a gate, take a gravel track signed 'Sheen' and 'Brund', which drops to a ford and footbridge across the **River Dove**. Follow the rising track for 100 metres then leave through a gate on the left from which a trod slants diagonally up the hill towards Sheen. Eventually, through a squeeze gate, the gradient briefly relents beside a broken

Through the water: *A track winds down to ford the shallow River Dove*

wall. However, after a few metres, watch for the buttresses of an old squeeze stile, through which the trod resumes its upward tack towards buildings at the top of the hill. More stiles take a contained path behind the buildings and between paddocks to emerge onto a lane.

7. Go left, but then at a bend, take the track off to **Harris Close Farm**. Passing through its gateway, a sign to 'Hartington' directs you right to a stile by a barn. Walk beside the barn to the field

beyond and carry on by the right-hand wall across successive fields. Where the wall eventually finishes, keep ahead to another stile. The way continues above a sheer grass bank and then a pine and larch plantation. Leaving over a stile at the far side, walk forward a few metres and then bear left past a waypost, losing height across a steep bank of gorse scrub. Over a stile at the bottom, follow a track to the right.

8. After 150 metres, leave through a wicket gate on the left and cross a field to a stiled bridge (the walkway may be problematic for dogs). Over the river, bear right to a small gate. Carry

on to find a squeeze stile just left of an indented wall corner and maintain the same direction across the next field to a gated stile.

Cut right to another stile and continue across a large pasture, corrugated by the ridges of medieval ploughing. At the far corner, pass through a wood and then a final meadow to come out onto a lane beside the **former cheese factory**. Walk left into the village and go right, back to the car park to complete the walk. ♦

Stilton cheese

Hartington Creamery — the cheese factory, was founded around 1870. As well as producing several local cheeses, it was one of only six dairies licensed to produce Blue Stilton cheese. The factory closed in May 2009, although the village Cheese Shop continued to operate. In 2012, a new creamery opened nearby producing five artisan cheeses including Peakland Blue, which is made to Hartington's original Stilton recipe.

Lyme Hall's stately Palladian front

Lyme Park

Wander through the park and woodlands of a 14th-century hunting estate

What to expect:
Moor and woodland paths, two short, energetic ascents

Distance/time: 5.5km/ 3½ miles. Allow 2 hours

Start: Lyme Park National Trust car park (fee)

Grid ref: SJ 963 823

Ordnance Survey Map: Explorer OL1 *The Peak District: Dark Peak area: Kinder Scout, Bleaklow, Black Hill & Ladybower Reservoir*

After the walk: Coffee shop and restaurant at Lyme Park

Walk outline

Beginning from the main car park, the walk climbs past the house to an unusual tower on Cage Hill. Rising determinedly to Lantern Wood, where a hillside belvedere overlooks the park, the way continues to the top of the moor and the stubs of two Saxon crosses. It is then downhill all the way back, exchanging distant views to Wales and the Pennines for more intimate woodland scenes and a glimpse of the deer park.

Lyme Park

Held by the Legh family for 600 years, the Lyme Park estate was gifted to the National Trust in 1946. The medieval house was rebuilt in the mid-16th century and part of its Tudor frontage was preserved in the centre of the 18th-century Palladian façade. Despite having one of the highest locations of any English grand house, the hall's interior decoration and furnishings lack nothing in elegance and beauty.

Not seen from the Park are terraced gardens overlooking an ornamental lake, a tranquil diversion after the rigours of a day spent hunting on the estate.

The Lantern

Red deer stag and hinds

Distant folly: *The Cage is framed by the roots of a veteran beech tree*

The Walk

1. A stepped path rises from the car park kiosk to the front entrance of **Lyme Hall**. *Lyme Park has featured in many television productions and films, perhaps its most famous role being that of Pemberley in the 1995 BBC adaptation of Jane Austen's Pride and Prejudice. The grand house adequately befits Darcy's income of more than £10,000 year, although it is said that Austen actually had Chatsworth in her mind's eye when writing the book.*

Displayed inside the hall is the Lyme Caxton Missal. One of the first books to be printed in two colours, it is the most complete copy of the work to survive, despite being forgotten for 300 years after being banned during the Reformation

Turn left, but where the drive then bends right, keep ahead up a grass bank. A path continues along a broad ridge to **The Cage**.

2. Turn around, but instead of retracing your outward path, bear slightly left. After 100 metres, fork left again on a trod that curves above a shallow grass fold to meet an estate drive in front of **Kennel Wood**. Follow the drive left for 300 metres then, approaching a circular fenced copse, veer off right across rough grass to a stile. Climb away on a trod that leads to a high ladder-stile across the wall bounding **Lantern Wood**.

3. A path heads away through the trees, soon passing a clearing containing the **Lantern**. *Built as a belvedere from which to enjoy the view to the house, The Lantern is a curious structure, changing in plan from square to octagonal as it rises. The upper storey and spire originally served as a bellcote on the northern gatehouse to the estate.*

Carry on to the far side of the wood, climbing out over another high ladder-stile onto the edge of the moor. Turn up beside the wall, briefly joining a track to a small quarry, but continuing beyond by the boundary to the top of the hill.

4. Ignore the stile and follow the wall along the ridge, the views being intermittently revealed as the ground rises and falls. The high spot is marked by a **memorial cairn** and topograph

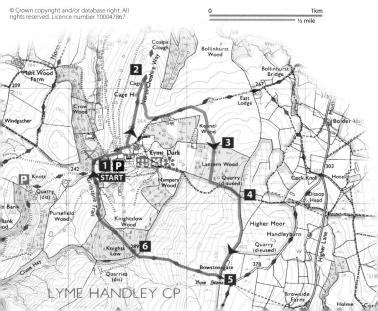

Dawn's early light: *Lyme Park*

indicating the surrounding landmarks. Stay with the continuing wall down to a ladder-stile and gate. Cross and walk out beside **Bowstonegate Farm** to meet the end of a lane, along which just to the left are the **Bow Stones**, set back in a small enclosure.

The Bow Stones are thought to be parts of two Saxon crosses. Such crosses were often erected to mark the boundary of a monastic estate or as waymarks at a crossing of moorland tracks. Those here are not necessarily in their original position and may have been discovered and placed

as a feature by Sir Piers Legh in the 16th century. Curiously, the stones are not the only examples of ancient twin crosses in the area; Robin Hood's Picking Rods can be seen roughly six miles to the north-east, below Cown Edge.

5. Return to the ladder-stile and now walk ahead down the moor on a developing track. There are glimpses across to The Cage and later, the mansion of Lyme Park, shyly hiding amongst the trees that surround it.

6. On reaching a junction in front of **Knightslow Wood**, pass through a gate and continue into the trees. Over

to the right a broad gap gives a view to an avenued enclosure in front of the house where fallow deer can often be seen grazing. A herd of red deer roam the wider estate and are perhaps best spotted early in the morning or evening when fewer people are about. Leave the far side of the wood and carry on at the edge of open grazing pasture beside a pinewood, passing through a final gate at the bottom to come out by the **car park** and thus complete the walk. ♦

A long hunting tradition

Situated on the fringe of Macclesfield Forest, hunting has always been a passion for Lyme's owners. The Cage was built in the 16th century as a hunting lodge since medieval times, but over the years it has been used as both a dwelling and a lockup. The Lantern, on the other hand, was erected purely to take advantage of the splendid view beyond the house across the Cheshire – Lancashire border.

The deep natural cleft of Lud's Church

Lud's Church

An intriguing forest gorge, once used as a secret meeting place by 14th-century religious dissidents

What to expect:
Generally clear forest and moorland paths

Distance/time: 10.5km/ 6½ miles. Allow 3½ hours

Start: Gradbach car park, on the narrow lane to Gradbach Mill

Grid ref: SJ 998 662

Ordnance Survey Map: Explorer OL24 *Peak District: White Peak area: Buxton, Bakewell, Matlock & Dove Dale*

After the walk: Café at Gradbach Mill (seasonal weekend opening), or The Ship Inn at Danebridge

Walk outline

From a riverside car park, the walk follows the Dane Valley past a former silk mill to Danebridge, where a nearby pub offers an inviting lunch stop. The return climbs onto the moor past a striking rock outcrop, the Hanging Stone, then drops into the trees to find the secluded defile of Lud's Church. The way continues through Forest Wood before finally descending along the steep flank of Black Brook's valley.

Lud's Church

A natural chasm formed by a landslip along the line of a geological fault, Lud's Church has always been a place of mystery. Sheer 15 metre-high walls thick with dripping moss and ferns contain a narrow passage some 100 metres long and, supposedly only on mid-summer's day does the sun shine full into the cleft. Pagans reputedly used it for solstice ceremonies, while Walter de Lud-Auk, a 14th-century follower of the religious dissident John Wycliffe, held secret services here, out of sight of the Catholic Church. Some say, too, that the place is the Green Chapel of Arthurian legend, where Sir Gawain encountered the Green Knight.

Clear signposts

Bilberries

The Walk

1. From the car park, follow the lane right, shortly bearing off to **Gradbach Mill**. Wind right and then left past the mill and café onto a riverside path. Continue at the edge of a field and then along a track. Reaching a sharp bend, cross a stone stile on the right and drop to a narrow footbridge spanning **Black Brook**.

2. Turn right past its confluence with the **River Dane**, bearing left onto a path contouring the woodland edge. Rising to a fork, keep right and carry on above the river.

3. Eventually, after crossing a stile, the path leaves the trees to cross a sloping meadow. Over another stile a fenced path runs between paddocks to **Back Forest Farm**. Crossing its drive, the ongoing path continues towards a second farm at **Back Dane**, which soon comes into view.

4. Meeting a track, fork right, but as it then swings to the buildings, keep ahead on a grass trod. The path meanders through a larch wood, in time dropping over a stile into a meadow. Bear left towards the river, picking up a track at the far end that rises to a lane beside **Dane Bridge**. Cross the bridge to visit the **Wincle Beer Company's brew house** (first track off on the left) and

Parting of the ways: *At its upper end, the mossy cleft of Lud's Church splits in two*

The Ship Inn, a short distance farther up the hill.

5. Return across the bridge and head up the lane, leaving after 100 metres along a path on the left signed to 'Back Forest' and 'Gradbach'. Crossing a drive, walk on between hedges and then at the bottom of a small field to enter a wood. Meeting another path, go right, climbing through a narrowing valley.

6. Emerging into open pasture, strike out to a wall stile just left of the far trees. Go right towards **Hangingstone Farm**, but immediately branch left on a rising path to a second stile. Signed right towards 'The Roaches', a track runs below the stark, fist-shaped outcrop of the **Hanging Stone**.

7. Reaching a junction, bear left of ahead along a concessionary path signed to 'Gradbach'. At the end, turn left in the direction of 'Lud's Church' along a moorland track. Keep on over the crest, the way gently descending beyond towards the fringe of **Forest Wood**.

Back Forest view: *Shutlingsloe dominates the horizon from the hill above Lud's Church*

Entering the trees, continue to a fork by an eye-catching outcrop.

8. Keep with the path ahead, but after 200 metres, beside a wooden rail, watch for a cleft in the rock wall bordering the path. Turn in and drop left into the ravine of **Lud's Church**.

Green with age, the dark, secret chasm of Lud's Church is the ideal setting for legend and tales of mystery infused with the supernatural and when tendrils of mist veil the trees above, you will swear that

you are not alone. Despite being far from Sherwood Forest, the ravine was one of the haunts of Robin Hood's band of outlaws. More sinisterly, it is said that a huntsman thrown by his horse from the lip above forever roams the forest shrouded in the moss and dead leaves on which he died, seeking revenge on lone travellers.

Walk through the deep gully, taking the right branch towards the far end, where more rugged steps climb out to the top.

9. Follow the path forward amongst the trees, shortly reaching a crossing path. Go right, towards 'The Roaches', the way wandering on through the forest. Ignore

a path later signed off onto the ridge and carry on until you reach a T-junction.

10. 'Gradbach and Danebridge' are indicated to the left. Bearing left at a later fork, continue across the steep valley side high above **Black Brook**.

Eventually the path falls to meet the stream at a ford. Remaining on this bank, carry on a little farther to a footbridge. Cross and retrace your outward steps past the **Gradbach Mill** to the car park to complete the walk. ♦

Gradbach Mill

The original 17th-century flax mill was rebuilt following a fire in 1785 and adapted to spin silk for what was then a growing local industry. But remoteness and the development of steam power rendered it uneconomic and, by 1875, the business had gone. The building later housed a sawmill and joinery shop before being converted into a youth hostel in 1984. It is now an outdoor education centre.

Chatsworth House enjoys an idyllic setting

Chatsworth

Walk in the woods and parkland surrounding one of Britain's grandest stately homes

What to expect:
Woodland and field paths; a stepped climb may be slippery when wet

---

Distance/time: 6.5km/ 4 miles. Allow 2-2½ hours

Start: Chatsworth House car park (fee)

Grid ref: SK 260 703

Ordnance Survey Map: Explorer OL24 *Peak District: White Peak area: Buxton, Bakewell, Matlock & Dove Dale*

After the walk: Licensed restaurants and cafés at Chatsworth

Walk outline

From the house, the walk climbs the wooded hillside to the 16th-century Hunting Tower. After visiting the lake, which supplies water to the grand fountain, it continues through the wood and along Dobb Edge. After dropping past Jubilee Rock, the route carries on across the deer park towards the River Derwent. The walk finally heads downstream to Queen Mary's Bower and Paine's Bridge, from there paralleling the main drive back to the house.

Chatsworth

Chatsworth has been home to the Cavendish family since 1549, when Sir William and his wife Bess of Hardwick bought the estate. After his death in 1553, Bess continued the work of building a grand house, although all that remains from her day is the Hunting Tower on the hill behind. The present hall has its origins in a rebuilding begun in 1687 by the 4th Earl (1st Duke) of Devonshire. It evolved into one of the finest stately mansions in the country and contains a wealth of fine furnishings and an impressive collection of art treasures.

Hunting Tower

Fallow doe and fawn

The Walk

1. From the top of the car park, take the drive signed 'Farmyard' and 'Playground'. Just before the farmyard entrance, slip through a gate onto the adjacent estate track and, directed by a sign 'Stand Wood Walks', continue up the hill. After 50 metres, rounding a bend, turn off onto a path on the left, which climbs through the trees to reach a higher track.

Cross to the ongoing path opposite, an occasionally muddy climb beside the gully of a stream that develops into a long flight of stone steps that may be slippery when wet. Emerging onto another track again, cross and go up beside the **Hunting Tower**, continuing along a short beech avenue to meet yet another track.

2. Turn right and then, at a fork, keep left, shortly reaching the tip of the **Emperor Lake**.

The Emperor Lake was created in 1843 to provide water for an immense fountain to celebrate a proposed visit by Tsar Nicholas I. Situated some 105 metres above the gardens, the eight-acre lake took just six months to complete, but in the event, the Tsar never arrived to see the magnificent spectacle. Capable of throwing a jet of water over 90 metres into the air, it was the highest fountain of its day and became the jewel of an already impressive water garden, created for the 1st Duke in the early 18th century.

Many features of that original garden have survived including the Cascade, a long flight of 24

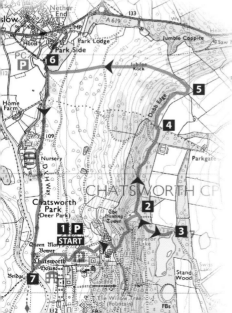

Sky mirror: *The Emperor Fountain and the south front of Chatsworth House*

steps down which water tumbles from the fountains of a 'water temple' presiding at its head, and the Canal Pond, a lake that extends south of the house for over 300 yards. There is also a fountain in the guise of a lifelike willow tree, which greatly impressed Celia Fiennes, a pioneering lady traveller who had no doubt seen it all in her journeys throughout the length and breadth of the country.

.3. Walk back to (**2**), but this time, carry on a little farther to a cross-roads. Turn right, the way signed 'Robin Hood'. Walk on through a conifer plantation, keeping ahead where the track later turns into a **timber yard**. Just before reaching a gate at the end, swing off left, following the wall to a high stile.

4. Over the stile, the signed path sticks by the wall over to the right, but an informal path follows the rim of **Dobb Edge** to take advantage of the spectacular views. However, be careful for there are some long drops. *In places the edge has been quarried and towards*

Grand design: *Chatsworth House is one of the nation's favourite stately homes*

the far end of the cliffs, the quarrymen have left a standing pillar beside which is an unfinished millstone.

As the edge runs out move back to the wall, where the path leads down to another high stile.

5. Instead of crossing, go left on a grassy swathe that descends with a shallow gully. Lower down, the path fragments, but keep heading forward at the edge of an open oak wood that has grown up amongst the boulders littering the apron below the edge. Aiming for a pair

of wooden field gates that soon become visible, continue downhill, passing a large boulder known as the **Jubilee Rock**, carved in commemoration of Queen Victoria's Diamond Jubilee.

Cross a stile beside the double gates and, over the track, walk in the same direction across more parkland, now following a sign to 'Baslow'. Reaching a high deer fence, follow it left around the perimeter of a wood to meet a path entering the estate through the **Cannon Kissing Gate** from the village.

6. Turn left along the clear path at the edge of the park. There is a glimpse of

the **River Derwent** tumbling over a weir as you shortly join an estate drive. Keep ahead at a junction by **White Lodge**, but after passing the cricket green you can move across to follow the water's edge. Approaching **Queen Mary's**

Bower, return to the track and pass through a gate to reach the main drive by **Paine's Bridge**. Cross the drive and swing left on a path that leads through a gate back up to the house and car park to complete the walk. ♦

Paine's Bridge

The accession of the 4th Duke saw many changes to the park and gardens, sweeping aside the 1st Duke's baroque gardens for the more naturalistic style championed by 'Capability' Brown. The successful Palladian architect James Paine, already working on new stables for the house, was commissioned to design a bridge across the river, which he sited to take best advantage of the view to the house.

The Hancocke graves, Eyam

Eyam

Discover the courageous story of a 17th-century lead-mining village devastated by the Plague

What to expect:
Field and woodland paths with quiet lanes; some steep climbs

Distance/time: 8km/ 5 miles. Allow 2½ hours

Start: Village car parks opposite Eyam Museum

Grid ref: SK 216 767

Ordnance Survey Map: Explorer OL24 *Peak District: White Peak area: Buxton, Bakewell, Matlock & Dove Dale*

After the walk: Pub and tea shops in Eyam

Walk outline

After wandering through Eyam the route climbs the hillside behind the village to visit an ancient spring. Descending through a wooded valley, the walk continues past the Riley Graves to explore the neighbouring spa of Stoney Middleton and its unusual church. The way back climbs beside old lead workings on the hillside above Middleton Dale, passing more sites associated with the plague as it returns to the village.

Eyam

Ever since the Black Death first ravaged Europe during the 14th century, plague was an intermittent occurrence. The Great Plague of 1664 was the last significant epidemic. It arrived at Eyam in 1665 in a bolt of cloth ordered by the village tailor, George Viccars. Once they realised what was happening, the villagers bravely imposed a quarantine and neighbouring settlements left food and supplies at the boundaries. Led by their priests, families managed as best they could, caring for the sick and burying the dead. Perhaps 75% of the community died and almost every old building has a tragic tale to tell.

Well dressing, Eyam

Brown hare

The Walk

1. Leaving the car park opposite the museum, walk down the hill and turn left at the bottom into the village. **Eyam Hall**, *passed on the left, is a fine Jacobean mansion, while on the green opposite are the* **village stocks** *and the* **Brick House***, formerly a pub known as the Stag's Parlour.*

Continue past a row of **Plague Cottages** and turn into the **churchyard**.

Originally dedicated to St Helen, it is now known as St Lawrence's and contains fine 16th-century wall paintings and a copy of the parish register listing the names of those who died during the terrible epidemic. *Outside is a fine sundial, a Celtic preaching cross and the tomb of Catherine Mompesson, wife of the rector who led the villagers through their ordeal.*

2. Walk past the church and go left along the eastern wall of the graveyard. *Passing the last of the old plots, look out for the fitting gravestone memorial to the Derbyshire and MCC cricketer Harry Bagshaw.* Leaving through a gate in the corner, walk on past the end of a playing field. Over a stile, continue up a meadow to pass through a gate beneath a **clump of beech trees**. Following a sign to 'Mompesson's Well', carry on uphill passing paddocks sometimes grazed by alpacas, to come out onto a lane.

3. Cross to a gate diagonally opposite and keep climbing on a stepped path through woodland. At the top, walk on to a gate and continue at the edge of a field above the trees. Through a small

Plague church?: *Eyam church, whose rector inspired the villagers during the Plague*

gate, bear diagonally up a couple of final fields to meet a lane. Go right and, in time reaching a junction, turn left. **Mompesson's Well** is then just a few metres along on the left.

4. Return to the junction, but now keep ahead, abandoning the lane a short distance farther on over a gap stile on the left into the edge of a wood. Signed 'Eyam', a rugged path descends steeply across the slope of a deep, narrow valley enclosing **Hollow Brook**. Emerging

onto the end of **Riley Back Lane**, walk down to the main road and turn left.

5. At the edge of the village, leave left up **Riley Lane**. Cresting the rise, bear right at a fork, shortly passing **Riley's Field** where, in a stone enclosure are the seven **graves of the Hancocke Family**. Return to the track and continue. At the next fork, keep right into woodland. Drop to a junction and go right again. The track falls steadily through the trees. Eventually leaving them behind, carry on between fields, finally coming out onto the bend of a lane.

Colourful meadows: *Old paths take the way back to Eyam*

6. Opposite, the track continues steeply downhill, the banks resplendent with wildflowers during summer. After passing a cemetery, the track widens to a lane and winds into Stoney Middleton past the '**Roman Baths**'.

While a Roman connection has never been proved, villagers long believed that the spring water could cure ailments, a reason why the church is dedicated to St Martin, patron saint of cripples. The spa baths were built during the late 18th century, but were never as popular as Buxton or Matlock.

Beyond the baths, the way swings left to the **church**.

7. Go right in front of the church to a junction and turn right again, climbing through the village. Where the street divides bear right and then keep left along **Cliff Bottom** past the **old pound**, once used to hold stray livestock but now serving as a small garden. Towards the top of the village, watch for a kissing-gate on the left, from which a path rises steeply away up a meadow. As the path eventually levels, walk on past a clump of trees to reach the **Boundary Stone**.

8. Keep going across the meadow and continue along an old walled path. Walk ahead beyond its end across a final meadow, from which a track ushers you into the village past an enclosure containing the **Lydgate Graves**.

9. Emerging in the centre of the village, bear left into **Church Street** and then keep right to retrace your steps past the church and **Eyam Hall** to complete the walk. ◆

The Boundary Stone

Without help from outside, the villagers could not have maintained their self-imposed quarantine and relied on food, medicines and other necessities from the surrounding settlements. The supplies were left at several points around the villages, such as the Boundary Stone and Mompesson's Well. In return, the Eyam villagers placed their coins for payment in the stone hollows, which were filled with vinegar to kill the contagion.

The view from Buxtors Hill to the distant hills of Lancashire

Forest Chapel

Through a royal hunting forest in the shadow of Cheshire's Matterhorn to a 17th-century chapel

What to expect:
Clear forest paths and tracks with some steep ascents

Distance: 9.5km/ 6 miles. Allow 3 hours

Start: Trentabank pay and display car park

Grid ref: SJ 961 711

Ordnance Survey Map: Explorer OL24 *Peak District: White Peak area: Buxton, Bakewell, Matlock & Dove Dale*

After the walk: Leather's Smithy

Walk outline

From the Trentabank Ranger Centre, the walk climbs through the forest onto Buxtors Hill. The route meanders on past the source of the River Bollin, then climbs again to reach the tiny settlement and church of Forest Chapel. After following an old hilltop trackway, the return enters the forest to describe a long and gradual descent into the Bollin valley. The final leg winds through the woods beside the Ridgegate Reservoir.

Macclesfield Forest

Established by the Normans, the Royal Forest of Macclesfield extended across the western Pennine foothills between the Goyt and Dane rivers. Set aside for the royal hunt, it comprised both woodland and rough moor. Today's forest lies within the upper Bollin valley; a working plantation producing timber, but also a haven for wildlife. Patches of deciduous woodland lie amongst the conifers and a small herd of red deer still roam free. Woodland birds flit amongst the trees while the reservoirs attract water birds, including grey herons, which breed beside Trentabank. Keep an eye open too for a herd of feral goats, which range around Buxtors Hill.

LEATHER'S SMITHY

Forest pub

Wild goat

The Walk

1. From the **Ranger Centre**, follow a path past the picnic area to a gap stile. Keep ahead parallel to the lane, but after a few metres, at the next junction, take the right fork towards Shutlingsloe. Ignore a track from the right and carry on to a fork. Follow the right branch, which climbs beside a wall, passing a viewpoint that looks back to the heronry. Over a crossing track, continue uphill for another 800 metres/½ mile to a squeeze gate and junction.

2. Remain with the track ahead, shortly reaching another divide. Keep left on the main path, from which a view across the valley to Tegg's Nose soon appears.

Although just outside the National Park's boundaries, **Tegg's Nose** is worth a visit to complete the day. *Its 380 metre summit offers fine views and the surrounding crags, woodland and moor attract a host of birds such as nuthatches, woodpeckers and tits. A Bronze Age burial site occupies the summit, which from the 16th century was quarried for its stone. The two small reservoirs beneath its foot were constructed in the 19th century to ensure a water supply for the mills in Langley.*

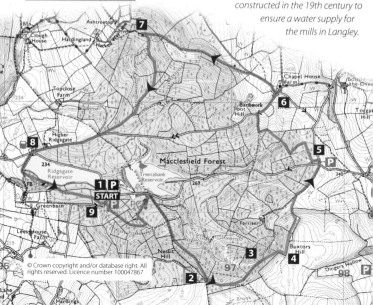

Night forest: *The stars swirl over Trentabank Reservoir on a cold winter's night*

3. At a fork by a well-placed seat, bear off right, climbing once more on a steep and intermittently stepped path, which can be slippery when wet. Crossing a broken wall, turn right at the edge of open scrub heath up the steep flank of **Buxtors Hill**.

There is a stunning panorama across the Cheshire Plain to the Welsh hills, while to the south east rises the distinctive summit of Shutlingsloe.

4. At the top, turn left in front of a stile along the short ridge. Occasional posts mark the descending path as it winds across a couple of broken walls before settling beside a fence. Carry on down to join a broad forest trail at the bottom and follow it right to a junction of lanes at **Standing Stone**, where a Saxon boundary or waymark cross once stood.

5. A few metres along the lane ahead, turn into a car park. Leave through a kissing-gate and curve right on a grass path. Bending left at a sign to 'Trentabank', it drops into the thick of

Hidden valley: *Forest plantations and reservoirs conceal the infant River Bollin*

the trees, eventually crossing a bubbling stream, the infant **River Bollin**. Continue on duckboards to a junction and turn right, regaining the height recently lost. Emerging onto a lane, turn uphill to **Forest Chapel's church**.

6. From the church, go back to the junction and turn right along an old hollow way. Reaching the corner of the forest, fork left through a gate into the trees. The path falls for 800 metres/½ mile to a junction near an abandoned barn.

Amongst the birds inhabiting the forest are buzzards, sparrowhawks and owls, which all prey on tiny mammals. Small birds such as tits, warblers and flycatchers are to be seen amongst the trees and the reservoirs attract wildfowl throughout the year including coot, great crested grebe, goldeneye, cormorant and geese.

7. Take the broad forest track down to the left, keeping right where it shortly splits. Continue steadily downhill, ultimately joining a lane, which in turn leads to a junction by **Leather's Smithy**.

8. Cross to the gated track opposite, which runs beneath the western

embankment of the **Ridgegate Dam**. Rounding the corner, carry on above the **River Bollin**'s deep valley. At a fork beyond the dam, keep left, passing new woodland planting above the lake before entering mature forest.

9. Reaching a lane, go left and then immediately right onto a track. Where it forks, take the left branch, which climbs to a broader forest trail. Turn left and walk back down to **Trentabank** to complete the walk. ♦

Forest Chapel

The lintel above the porch carries two date stones, one for its founding in 1673 and the other commemorating the rebuilding in 1834. Its pleasing, outer simplicity is mirrored inside, where a charity board records details of Mr Edmund Brough's bequest to the poor of the parish. St Stephen's is one of the few churches to celebrate renewal in a rush-bearing service each August.

Chimney and derelict engine house at the Magpie Mine

The Magpie Mine

Derbyshire's best-preserved lead-mining remains and three lovely dales

What to expect:
Field and woodland paths; some steep climbs

Distance/time: 9km/ 5½ miles. Allow 3 hours

Start: White Lodge pay and display car park beside the A6, Taddington Dale

Grid ref: SK 170 706

Ordnance Survey Map: Explorer OL24 *Peak District: White Peak area: Buxton, Bakewell, Matlock & Dove Dale*

After the walk: The Cock and Pullet, Sheldon

Walk outline

Leaving the car park, the walk climbs through Deep Dale. Towards the top, it runs across fields to Sheldon and on to the Magpie Mine. Returning, the route passes the village pub to descend a deep gorge below Little Shacklow Wood. Entering Wye Dale, the way turns upstream beside pastures and the edge of Great Shacklow Wood. Later climbing into the trees, it eventually meets the outward path at the foot of Deep Dale.

The Magpie Mine

The Magpie Mine stands on a rich lattice of lead ore veins worked from around 1740 onwards. It was one of several pits exploiting the seams and competition was fierce, with miners breaking into adjacent tunnels to sabotage the workings. Tragedy struck in 1833 when three men in the neighbouring Maypitt Mine suffocated after Magpie workers lit an underground fire to drive them out. The surface ruins are dominated by an engine house and chimney built in 1869 to accommodate a Cornish steam engine, while the pithead cage and winding gear dates from an attempt to re-open the mine in the 1950s.

Old hand winch

Magpie

Industrial heritage: *Ruined steam engine house and chimneys at the Magpie Mine*

The Walk

1. Leave the car park by the pay station along a path signed 'Ashford' and 'Taddington'. After crossing a couple of sloping meadows the path turns up the bed of a trickling, lime-rich stream. A little way up, climb a stile on the left and continue between outcrops of limestone into the broader, flower-rich meadows of the valley above.

2. Reaching a junction, go right into

Deep Dale, the path rising at the edge of an open wooded meadow. As the path gains height, the valley narrows, bordered by steep meadow, screes and high, rugged cliffs. The path draws beside the stream, which later switches onto the other side of the wall.

3. A short distance beyond, pass through a gate to continue on the other side of the wall. After another 30 metres, watch for a stile and cross back. Climb away up the hillside to another stile at the top. Walk on by the left perimeter at the edge of successive pastures towards the ruins of the Magpie Mine, now seen in the middle distance. In time, the left boundary angles away and then back, the trod leading to a stile by a power cable post. Go right to a squeeze stile and walk across a final field to emerge over a stile beside a gate onto a lane.

4. Turn left towards **Sheldon**. Rounding a bend, cross the green on the right to a stile and gate beside a cottage, from which a path is signed 'Magpie Mine'. Walk through a small paddock and over a stile into the corner of a field. Head away at a shallow angle to another stile in the far corner, beyond which, follow the dogleg wall left to a squeeze stile.

5. Entering an enclosure at the head of a track, take the gate opposite and strike a right diagonal across a couple of fields to the **Magpie Mine**.

6. After exploring the impressive ruins, return to the head of the track (**5**) and follow it right through a succession of fields. Entering a final field before a farm, abandon the track, moving left to a stile behind a large corrugated shed. Bear left across a small area of grass to a second stile beside a **dew pond**. Cross the bottom of a small field to yet another stile, the path ultimately leading out into the **village**. Follow the lane right past the pub, the **Cock and Pullet**.

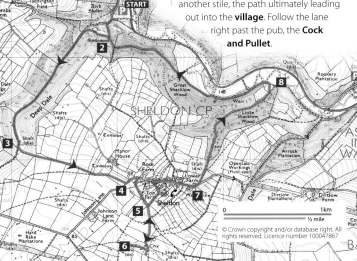

Deep Dale in spring: *Cowslips and orchids spangle the limestone meadows in May*

7. At the far side of the village, just past **Lower Farm**, leave the lane through a squeeze gap on the left. Head downfield, keeping with the lower of two paths along the base of the deepening valley. Bypassing a gate at the entrance to a small water treatment plant, the continuing path passes through a couple of gates into dense woodland. Becoming rugged, it drops steeply through **Nettler Dale** below **Little Shacklow Wood**, passing workings dug in search of prized

Derbyshire Black Marble. Beyond the quarries, the valley broadens, becoming meadow as it meets **Wye Dale**.

8. Reaching a junction of paths, turn left beside a wall. Beyond a couple of meadows the path passes into woodland by the substantial remains of an **old mill**, used to crush bones for the manufacture of fertiliser. The path bypasses the buildings on the left, following the leat that fed the waterwheels back to a weir on the river.

A little farther on, the path passes above a stream gushing from a hole in the rock, the outlet of **Magpie Sough** which

drains the mine. Passing **fishponds**, the path moves away from the river behind meadows, rising gently into the trees to a junction. Keep ahead, now climbing more determinedly above a steep slope. The way eventually falls to a gate and another junction. Remain with the path ahead, which now descends through hazel coppice. At the bottom (**2**), turn right and retrace your outward route to the car park to complete the walk. ♦

Deep Dale wildlife

A designated Site of Special Scientific Interest, the valley is rich in wildflowers, with cowslips, early purple orchids and meadow saxifrage bringing delicate colour in early summer. Later, lily of the valley, bird's nest orchid and rock rose are to be found, while towards the end of summer, Devil's-bit scabious and grass of Parnassus are common. Amongst the butterflies that may be seen are dark green fritillary, green hairstreak and dingy skipper.

Torside Reservoir

Longdendale

Along the course of one of the first trans-Pennine railways with views across a reservoir

What to expect:
Clear tracks and paths, little climbing

Distance/time: 7km/ 4½ miles. Allow 2 hours

Start: Torside pay and display car park, beside B6105

Grid ref: SK 068 983

Ordnance Survey Map: Explorer OL1 *The Peak District: Dark Peak area: Kinder Scout, Bleaklow, Black Hill & Ladybower Reservoir*

After the walk: The Peels Arms at Padfield

Walk outline

Despite the main road through Longdendale, the steeply rising edges on either flank give the narrow valley a wild and rugged character. From the car park, the walk follows the line of the former railway west, before crossing the valley on the Torside Dam. Woodland paths take the way back above the opposite shore, eventually breaking out to the open moss at the lake head. After re-crossing beneath the Woodhead Dam, the return is along another stretch of the old railway.

Longdendale

Approached by long valleys from both sides, Woodhead has long been a conduit for travellers and goods crossing the Pennines. In the Middle Ages, teams of packhorses carried salt from Cheshire and the same route was followed in 1731 by an early turnpike. The road remains and, while susceptible to closure during winter snow, part of it is still the main route between Lancashire and Yorkshire. One of the first trans-Pennine railways was routed along the valley too, although it avoided the summit by burrowing through the hill. The trackbed now carries the Trans Pennine Trail, which runs 207 miles coast to coast between Southport and Hornsea.

Below Hey Edge

Short-eared owl

The Walk

1. A winding easy-access trail and more direct cycle path and bridleway climb past a memorial woodland behind the car park. At the top is the course of the former railway. Follow it to the right.

Running between Sheffield and Manchester, the line opened in 1845 to transport coal from Yorkshire. The tunnel was the longest of its kind at the time. However, hard-working engines produced heavy smoke and the confined conditions made life almost intolerable for the driver and fireman and, by the 1930s, electrification was seen as the answer.

2. After some 1.6 kilometres/1 mile the track meets the road. Cross and go right. Ignore the first left (the continuation of the **Trans Pennine Trail**) and instead, take the second sharp turning a few

metres farther on, signed the 'Pennine Way'. The track drops below the embankment to swing across the dam of the **Torside Reservoir.**

3. At the far side, curve left over the overflow channel, but then leave up steps on the right. Cross a leat and, ignoring the track off to the left, climb forward through a gate. To the right, a path leads through the trees above the northern bank of the reservoir. Later passing through a gate, the path turns up towards the main road. However, go through a kissing-gate on the right into **Tinsel School Wood** to follow a concessionary path signed to 'Torside'. In time leaving the trees, the path falls to a **footbridge** over the leat and eventually closes with the shore. After crossing a bridge over the foot of **Crowden Brook**, the path turns from the lake.

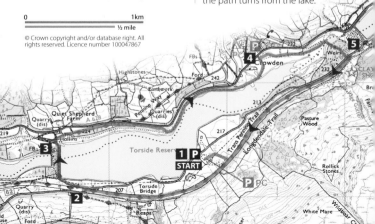

0   1km

½ mile

© Crown copyright and/or database right. All rights reserved. Licence number 100047867

Rock and water: *Torside Reservoir*

4. Before the road, swing through a kissing-gate on the right and join another leat towards the **Woodhead Dam**. Beyond the head of the lake, the path leads to a footbridge across the overflow from the reservoir above. Cross to the other side of the valley and follow the service drive up through the trees to the road.

5. Cross to a path opposite, which climbs left back to the old railway track. Turn right and follow it for 1.6 kilometres/1 mile to the point at which you first joined it. Drop right back to the **Torside car park** to complete the walk. ♦

The lost river

The River Ethrow, which flows via the Goyt into the Mersey, is now largely lost within the chain of reservoirs stepping down the valley. Woodhead was begun first in 1847, but because of construction difficulties was the last to be completed. With Torside, Rhodeswood and, tucked to one side, Arnfield, it supplies drinking water to Manchester, while Valehouse and Bottoms keep water flowing downstream in the lower Ethrow.

Useful Information

Visit Peak District & Derbyshire

The Peak's official tourism website covers everything from accommodation and special events to attractions and adventure. www.visitpeakdistrict.com

Peak District National Park

The Peak District National Park website also has information on things to see and do, plus a host of practical details to help plan your visit. **www.peakdistrict.org**

Visitor Centres

The main TICs provide free information on everything from accommodation and transport to what's on and walking advice..

Bakewell	01629 816558	bakewell@peakdistrict.gov.uk
Castleton	01629 816572	castleton@peakdistrict.gov.uk
Moorland Centre	01433 670207	edale@peakdistrict.gov.uk
Upper Derwent	01433 650953	derwentinfo@peakdistrict.gov.uk

Local Museums

To learn more about the Peak District's long and varied history, visit:
www.visitpeakdistrict.com/see-and-/museum-heritage.aspx

Buxton Museum and Art Gallery

Varied and interesting local museum looking at everything from fossils and Romans to railways. **www.derbyshire.gov.uk/leisure/buxton_museum** | **01629 533540** | **buxton.museum@derbyshire.gov.uk**

Derby Museum and Art Gallery, The Strand, Derby, DE1 1BS

Collections and displays exploring Derbyshire's history, culture and natural environment. **www.derby.gov.uk/leisure-and-culture/museums-and-galleries** | **01332 641901** | **info@derbymuseums.org**

Bus Travel

Peakland's towns and many of the villages are served by bus. Information is available from Traveline on 0871 200 22 33 or **www.traveline.info**

Weather

Online weather forecasts for the Peak District are available from the Met Office at **www.metoffice.gov.uk/loutdoor/mountainsafety/** and the Mountain Weather Information Service at **www.mwis.org.uk/**